THE SWAN, LEATHERHEAD
and its
BREWERY

THREE HUNDRED YEARS OF HISTORY

THE SWAN, LEATHERHEAD
and its
BREWERY

Mary Rice-Oxley

ISBN 0 9506009 8 9

Published by
  Leatherhead & District Local History Society
  64 Church Street
  Leatherhead
  KT22 8DP

Front cover: The Swan Hotel, c1900

Back cover: Token minted by Edward Shales, early 17th century

Printed by J W Arrowsmith Ltd., Bristol.

Contents

List of Illustrations

Preface

The information gathered in this history has come from many sources. The annual Proceedings of the Leatherhead & District Local History Society and its other publications have been invaluable, as have been a large number of other sources too numerous to list.

I am most grateful to the Society, particularly Jack Stuttard, for their co-operation in the production. Many of the photographs are from their archives, and Stephen Fortescue has also generously made other photographs available to me. I was particularly pleased to be lent the original of the unique view of the Brewery, owner unknown, which was found being used as a cupboard back!

I would also like to thank the Brewery History Society for their support and encouragement during the writing of this history.

Reference has been made to –

Through Stuart Britain. The Adventures of John Taylor, the Water Poet. Edited and selected by John Chandler, 1999.

East Surrey by 'Bell Street' – this being a history of the East Surrey Traction Co. Ltd. 1974.

The Reigate Brewery – research by Richard Symonds. These papers are at the Surrey History Centre at Woking.

Turville – The Life and Times of Turville Kille, 1998.

Mary Rice-Oxley 2001.

Introduction

The year 1936 saw the closure and demolition of a famous Leatherhead landmark after three centuries to make way for a commercial development.

From its beginning as an inn, the Swan grew to a large hotel with an important part to play in the social life of the town.

The inn stood at the north-eastern corner of the crossroads in the centre of the town on land owned by the Manor of Thorncroft.

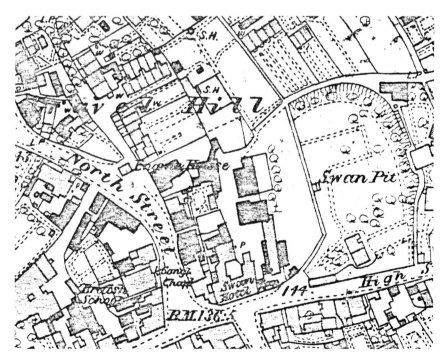

Map of Leatherhead, 1868, showing the Swan Hotel with its gardens in the Swan Pit. The buildings in the Swan yard are those of the early brewery

Reproduced from Ordnance Survey map, Crown Copyright

Behind it, in the common field, was a marl-pit. Until the mid seventeenth century the marl, or chalk, would have been taken by cart to the farms to enrich the heavy local soil. Later this area was to be known as the Swan Pit and was used as a sheltered spot for sheep pens.

Early History

The first written reference to the Swan was in 1636 in a poem by John Taylor, who is usually referred to as 'the water poet'. He was a self-educated Thames wherryman turned pamphleteer and writer of verse. He also undertook twelve journeys round the country publishing accounts of these. In 1631 he travelled through Surrey when it could be presumed that he visited the Swan for he described the River Mole running underground and rising at Norbury.

There is, however, a reference in the archives of the Leatherhead and District Local History Society to 'William Tanner's Swan Mark, 1574', which may be taken to refer to the Swan, Leatherhead, and an early seventeenth century innkeeper, Edward Shales, had the right to mint his own tokens which were used for currency at the time.

By 1637, the Swan was owned by Thomas Goodman and was in the tenancy of a 'Miss' Brown. It included a property called Bishopps which is thought to have adjoined the Swan to the east in the High Street. This house is again referred to in 1713 as 'adjoining the Swan Inn, in the occupation of Thomas Nettlefold and now of Henry Loveland, a cordwainer'.

On 29th of January 1667, John Evelyn, the diarist who lived at Wotton, wrote 'that there hung some years ago, and perhaps may still hang upon the walls of the Swan Inn at Leatherhead in Surrey, a picture of four children, dates of birth between 1610 and 1650, of whom a lad about the age of young Evelyn is represented in a coat reaching to his ankles'. This was probably one of several pictures supposed to have been bought from Randalls in Leatherhead which stood on the road to Cobham. The two boys were aged about twelve and fourteen, the girls younger. John Sands, whose family owned Randalls from 1522–1716, had six children named Thomas, Francis, Jane, Mary, Ann and Elizabeth.

THE SWAN HOTEL, LETHERHEAD.

The Situation of this beautiful Village is too well known to require much comment, as it is presumed to stand unrivalled for its views and delightful rural retirement. Letherhead is 4 miles from Epsom, 5 from Dorking, and 3 from the far-famed Box-Hill. To the admirer of Nature, Geologist, or the disciples of Isaac Walton, Letherhead and its immediate neighbourhood hold out many inducements, and the quick transit which may be made by Railway to the Metropolis, render it most desirable to persons seeking health or change of air.

WILLIAM MOORE

respectfully intimates that the different Suites of Apartments will be found so arranged as to combine comfort and retirement, while he pledges himself to be ever assiduous in most scrupulously attending to his patrons expressed wishes.

An excellently supplied Larder. Choice Wines and Piquant Liqueurs.

POST HORSES & CARRIAGES. Superior LOCK-UP COACH HOUSES.

BILLIARDS.

Agent by appointment to the South-Western Railway Company.

Advertisement for the Swan Hotel, c.1860

In 1668 a survey of Leatherhead gives figures for accommodation for men and horses in the town at the Bull, the Swan and the Running Horse being enough beds for eleven people and sufficient stabling for eighteen horses.

In the early 1700's Edward Toy was the owner of the Swan, and also the King's Head which was further up the High Street on the opposite side.

On 11th of February 1705 a Chancery Court was held at the Swan to deal with the inheritance of Edward Toy's wife Sarah

14

whose father, George Rouse, had died intestate. George Rouse, called by Samuel Pepys 'the Queens' Tailor', had lived in the house in Ashtead Park, subsequently occupied by the Headmaster of the City of London Freemen's School. In 1812 Edward Toy's grandson, Richard Toy, left £1,200 for monthly grants for six poor and aged persons in Leatherhead.

By 1680, stage-coaches and carriers were calling at the Swan. In 1791, the coach from the Golden Cross, Charing Cross, left at 7 a.m. each day on its way to Surrey. Every day also, excepting Sunday, the Brighton Coach left the Swan at 2 p.m. The post was taken by the mail coach for London at 10 p.m. nightly.

In the 'Directory' for 1791 the Inn is described as a 'very genteel house with good accommodation, most excellent stabling and good post chaises with able horses for hire'. Trout from the River Mole was one of the specialities served and Pepys recorded earlier having sampled the dish.

On 4th October 1806 an inquest was held at the Swan into the unfortunate death of Miss Harriet Mary Cholmondley in an accident at the Swan corner. An open barouche landau in which she was travelling with the Princess of Wales and Lady Sheffield turned over. The injured ladies were taken to the Swan by Mr. Jones the innkeeper.

During renovations at the Swan in 1922 one of Mr. Jones business cards was found behind the fireplace in a room beside the bar. Dated Jan. 9th 1815 it read 'Swan Inn, Leatherhead. John Jones begs leave to return his sincere and grateful thanks to the nobility, gentry and public in general for their distinguished support and encouragement since he commenced business for himself, and further to acquaint them with considerable satisfaction that the present reduction in the price of corn enables him to run good and able horses (with neat post chaises) at 15d. per mile'.

Soon after this time, a memorial tablet was set into the wall in the Swan yard which read 'Near this spot lies poor Jack, a pony late the property of Mr. Joseph Hemsley of this Inn who was shot the 30th day of April 1833 in the 42nd year of his age'.

By local tradition, the sum of one penny was charged for permission to bring a corpse through this yard to prevent a right of way being established – the yard was a short cut from the Kingston Road end of Leatherhead to the church.

The Victorian Years

By the year 1838 daily coaches ran through Leatherhead to Arundel, Bognor and Worthing. As many as eight coaches stopped at the Swan every day except Sunday. The horses were changed by the ostlers in the yard to a fresh set of four, and within half an hour the coach would be on its way. On May Day and other festive occasions the coachman's whipstock would be decorated with ribbons and flowers and the horses with coloured rosettes. The 'Accommodation' coach went to Worthing, arriving half an hour before the 'Sovereign'. The 'Comet' went to Bognor. 'The Star' left London for Horsham mid-afternoon, reaching Leatherhead in the early evening. 'The Times' ran to Guildford, arriving in Leatherhead late in the day.

The stage-coaches were coloured yellow, black or blue with gold trimmings carrying four inside and often eleven or twelve outside. Travelling at ten miles an hour the horses were changed every ten miles. With coaches running punctually the new horses were ready to change while warm drinks were served to passengers in the Inn during the half-hour halt.

Coaches served Leatherhead well into the 1840's and still eight a day were calling in 1845. However, by this time the railways were reaching out from London to the coast, and Leatherhead had its first railway in 1859. Private coaches were still calling at the Swan which, of course, had its own fly that met all trains at the local station.

The Post Office introduced a new mail-coach service from 1887 to avoid the heavy dues on parcels imposed by the railway. A court case in March 1889 charged a Swan Hotel ostler with mishandling the horses of the mail vans which passed through Leatherhead every night to Guildford. With the new century motor vans and motor cars took over from the horse-drawn vehicles.

In 1858 the Swan became the property of William Moore and, on his death in 1865, passed to his wife Emily, staying in the family

The earliest photograph of the Swan, c.1865, taken by Leatherhead photographer, Austin Youell

until 1898. During this time the Swan became a first-class hotel with extensive stabling and the Moore family's reputation, especially that of Miss Emily Moore, their daughter who ran the hotel after her father's death, was widespread. Suites of apartments were available. 'Quiet comfort, good food and drink' were advertised, as were the floral arrangements.

Behind the hotel were very lovely gardens where the original marl-pit had been, with greenhouses to grow the flowers for decoration and with a vegetable garden for supplies for the hotel restaurant. By the garden was a cow-yard where Miss Moore bred prize Jersey and Alderney cows. Each cow had its name above its stall and every day the fourteen to eighteen cows could be seen going to their pastures at Thorncroft and Downside through the High Street and Church Street to return in the evening.

The young Princess of Teck, a relative of Queen Mary, the actress Ellen Terry and the singer Jenny Lind were among the well-known visitors, many of whom returned again and again. A resident for six months was the artist Cecil Aldin who specialised in hunting scenes. Miss Moore not only gave him his first commission, but also provided him with a studio. Banquets, receptions and dances were held in the ballroom at the hotel or at the Victoria Hall further up the High Street with music provided by

A view of the Swan with the High Street beyond before the building of the Brewery in 1874

The same view in 1895. The brewery offices can be seen to the right of the hotel.

The hotel was particularly imposing when approached from Church Street, c.1900

the Blue or Red Hungarians in their gay Hussar uniforms. The ballroom was lit by candlelight and at some time the ballroom floor had to be shored up as part of the archway leading from the road below it was becoming unstable. The ballroom, or Assembly Room as it was later known, was refurbished in 1862.

Miss Moore also catered for outside events, including race meetings at Epsom, Sandown, Kempton and Hurst Park, also for functions at Fetcham Park Polo Club. At the yearly sale of Queen Victoria's horses in the Paddock at Hampton Court she provided luncheon in a huge marquee and was always visited there by Edward, Prince of Wales. The food was also arranged for Mr. Pantia Ralli of Ashtead Park for his staff's annual celebration in a marquee in his grounds. The Mid-Surrey Fox Hunt or Stag Hunt, with their pack of hounds, would sometimes meet at the Swan, the ladies wearing long habits, riding side-saddle, and the gentlemen either scarlet or blue frock-coats with white breeches, top boots, top hats or peaked velvet caps.

On New Year's Eve the townspeople danced in the streets and on New Year's Day a dance was held at the hotel which anybody could attend. When the endless traffic of racegoers to the Epsom Summer Race Meeting had lessened in the evenings, a group of buskers entertained the crowd in the street in front of the hotel.

The Brontë family, especially Charlotte, had connections with Abraham Dixon of Cherkley Court and on 28th November 1881 a

Brontë family gave a concert at the hotel, but whether they were related to Charlotte is not known. Mr. and Mrs. F. Brontë and their four children, Constance, Ernest, Minnie and Edith, took part. They danced a quadrille and a polka, sang duets, played a trio for flute, violin and piano and the whole family completed the programme with a performance of Haydn's Surprise Symphony.

Another auspicious occasion at the hotel in December 1891 was a presentation to Sir David Evans, the recently elected Lord Mayor of London, of his portrait in recognition of his five year mastership of the Surrey Farmers Hunt.

The Swan Brewery had been started in 1859 by William Moore and greatly increased the family's influence in the town, the Brewery premises being adjacent to the hotel on its eastern side, up the High Street. Surrey beer was described as 'very yeasty and new – rarely more than four days old'.

The Swan Hotel stayed in the Moore family until 1898 when it was sold for £13,300 with 60 years' lease to George Brown. Miss Emily Moore retired to live at Kingston House, which stood at the top of Bull Hill, outside which John Wesley is reputed to have given his last sermon. Here she lived until her death in 1930.

The Early 20th Century

After the Moore family sold the Swan Hotel it continued as a first class hotel under several owners, at the centre of an increasingly busy town, its Assembly Room still being used for so many functions.

A booklet published by the hotel around this time includes a hotel tariff showing a double bedroom at 5/- per night, a sitting room 5/- per day, a fire in either between 6d. and 1/6, a cold hip bath 6d. or a hot one 1/-. A breakfast was 2/6 and a cold luncheon 2/6, hot lunch 2/6. A choice at tea-time, priced 2/6, of eggs or meat, fish 1/- or 2/-. Dinner was 3/6.

In the Swan Tap, the equivalent of the public bar, a pint of beer cost 1½d. or 2d. with a clay pipe included in the price for regular

Coronation celebrations for King Edward V11 in 1902. The hotel, the High Street and Church Street were decorated with flags and bunting

Miss Emily Moore, famous for her hospitality at the Swan, aged 82

customers. Later in the 1920's the Tap was called the 'Swan Shades'

In January 1908 a bad fire broke out at Moulds, the iron-mongers situated just above the Swan in the High Street. Six horses were stabled in the rear of the building; these were rescued, led round to the Swan Pit and taken to safety in the Swan's stables.

During Mr. Davy's time as landlord, a party of revellers took the plaster statues which stood round the Assembly Room. They were found next morning placed at intervals on both sides of the High Street!.

The Swan garden with James Ginger, the gardener, during the Moore family's ownership

James Ginger feeding the pigs in the farmyard behind the hotel

The hotel stable and garage, c.1908

The hotel yard, c.1910, with a view through to the High Street

The Leatherhead Unionist Club Dinner in the Assembly Room of the hotel. March 23rd 1919

By this time the railways were increasing in popularity, and the first bus service to Kingston was in 1911. A few well-to-do still travelled by private stage coach, among whom was the American millionaire Alfred Vanderbilt, often driving his own coach, the 'Venture', calling at the Swan on the journey from London to Brighton. He lost his life when the Lusitania was torpedoed in May 1915.

In 1921 a new route between Epsom and Guildford for the East Surrey Traction Co. was started, and the two buses used were outstationed at the Swan yard. Later, this was increased to four. The practice of keeping buses in open yards attached to public houses arose because suitable sites for new garages had to be assessed after some operating experience on the routes, and also allowance had to be made for the length of time to be taken in the building of the garages.

By 1923 a maximum of six buses could be parked at the Swan, used on the 408 bus route. Any extra vehicles needed at weekends were parked in the yard at the Bull Hotel in Station Road. By 1924 the new bus garage had been built on land formerly farmed by Mizens beyond the River Mole. This was demolished in 1999 and the site redeveloped.

Steps to Closure

During the post First World War period the hotel changed owners several times but always gave good service to visitors and local people alike, but finally, in 1934, came into the ownership of George Laceby who was only there for two years. He had bought it for £520 with a 22 year lease to run – this being the end of a 100 year tied tenancy to Mellersh & Neale. He moved into the Swan with his wife and two small children. The family sitting room was on the first floor, above the front door; this had an old sloping floor, necessitating propping up the furniture with wedges. The older daughter describes the ballroom as being huge, dim and echoing. Mrs. Laceby was keen to present some of the public rooms on the ground floor to their best advantage and spent a

An unknown group on an outing pose for their photograph outside the Swan, c.1918–20

A private coach outside the Swan, c.1928, photographed by Albert
Warren of The Crescent, Leatherhead

The Swan Hotel in 1929. The name 'The Swan Shades' can be seen
above the door at the far end of the building

The back entrance to the hotel, c.1930

great deal of time and energy treating the old red brick floors, putting the hearths into working order and cleaning the copper and brasswear.

There was garaging for 30 cars, the banqueting room sat 115, the restaurant 40. The restaurant, reached through the 'Winter Garden', was panelled and had a massive fireplace, beside which perched a parrot. By this time there were no horses left, but there was a car-hire service with a 'chauffeur' and the cars were black Daimlers.

George Laceby, after his purchase, found that there was a schedule of dilapidations of over £1,000, but also that the tied tenancy was for all malt liquors at £13 per barrel, whereas the cheapest beer at that time was about £75 per barrel. He approached Col. Neale of the brewery for a fulfilment of the deed, but both this and

The hotel yard seen through the archway from the High Street, c.1930

The High Street, c.1930, with an AA patrolman directing the traffic

The Winter Garden, c.1934

One of the hotel Daimlers, c.1934

The last photograph of the Swan due for demolition. September 1936

an offer to sell back the lease for £6,000 were refused. An offer to consult King's Counsel, Sir W. Jowitt, abide by his decision and pay half his fee was also refused. A private consultation with the K.C. costing £50 found in Mr. Laceby's favour. Again the brewery refused, and Mr. Laceby then gave notice that he would obtain his beer supplies elsewhere, leaving Col. Neale and the brewery to take what action they wished against him. As another form of attack he commissioned an architect to draw up plans to demolish the hotel and rebuild it in a position further back on the garden side. This he leaked out so that the brewery would know he was in earnest – although for the cost of £20,000 he had no intention of carrying it out.

Earlier he had been approached by Healey & Baker, the London property dealers, who wished to purchase the Swan for clients unnamed. He stated that he had no wish to sell. They then asked if he would give an indication of the sum involved if he changed his mind, the figure being given as £21,000. There was no further action by the brewery and Mr. Laceby continued to build up the Swan trade, particularly the catering for the largest functions of up to 115 persons. There was little profit, but all his home and personal expenses were taken by the hotel accounts – his family had by then moved into a private house in the town. After some time he opened up talks with the London agents,

The High Street, c.1960. Barclays Bank, originally the Brewery offices, was replaced by the entrance to the Swan Centre in 1981.

undertaking to sell at £17,500. Some three months elapsed with no communication with the buyers who had been expected to sign the contract agreement. He then offered the business to a London brewery at a lower figure with a four-day limit on their acceptance. However, luck was with him for on the third day he received the signed contract agreement. The buyers were revealed as Burtons, the tailors, who said they were not interested in the contents or the buildings of the property, so all the furniture and pewter fittings were sold, and even the iron framework of the large garage went to a London metal dealing firm. Some of the items of copperware and plate were kept by the family, as were two of the large mirrors from the Assembly Room. Despite protests, the sale in September 1936 resulted in the demolition of the hotel and the redevelopment of the whole site, a turning point in the development of modern Leatherhead.

The large white Swan which had been mounted above the hotel entrance porch was brought back to Leatherhead in 1990 from a garden in Fetcham where it had been since the demolition. It was refurbished and is now in the garden of Leatherhead Museum, a reminder of part of the town's historic past.

Particulars of the Swan Hotel, Leatherhead 1898

The auction of the hotel took place at 'The Mart', Tokenhouse Yard, City, on Monday 5th September 1898, the auctioneers being White & Sons of Dorking and Leatherhead. The sale particulars included the following details:

The Swan Hotel, Leatherhead, Surrey. In this most beautiful neighbourhood, in the centre of the Village, at the Junction of the Main Roads from London and Kingston to Guildford, Dorking and Horsham, within 20 miles from London by Road, and about 5 minutes from the Leatherhead Stations, L.B. & S.C. & L. & S. W. Railways, from whence the City and West End are reached in just over 30 minutes.

Good livery yard & Jobmaster's business

Extensive stabling & coachhouses; ample outbuildings, good garden and Hotel Tap, at a Rental of £100 per annum.

It has for more than 50 years past been carried on under the management of the same family, during which time it has justly obtained the reputation of being one of the Best Hotels in the Home Counties.

The Hotel which is old-fashioned and attractive externally, and also internally from its arrangement and home-like appearance contains the following accommodation:

GROUND FLOOR

Private Sitting-room 15-ft. 3-in. by 13-ft. 6-in., with separate Entrance and Passage-way from the Street

Sitting-room 15-ft. 3-in. by 12-ft. 6-in.

Main Entrance to Hotel with Bar and Bar Parlour

Smoking Room 16-ft. by 16-ft.

A very attractive Sitting Room in two divisions, communicating with the Bar Parlour and with an Entrance also to the Conservatory and Coffee Room, the full size of which is 18-ft. 3-in. by 14-ft. 10-in.

Conservatory 15-ft. by 12-ft. and Entrance From Yard

Handsome Coffee Room with Hooded Fireplace and Serving Hatch, the joinery and beams being of pitch pine; the ceiling is lofty and the size 28-ft. 6-in. by 17-ft. 6-in.

Lavatory adjoining

Close to the Bar and Coffee Room is an enclosed Larder with Sliding Glazed Sashes and Tiled Floor and Sides, for the use of the Coffee Room attendant, under which and the Stairs are convenient enclosed Cupboards

W.C. at Foot of Stairs

Still Room. Passage Room leading to Kitchen and Entrance to Offices, used for cleaning plate, knives, boots etc.

Tradesman's Porch Entrance from Yard.

Larder. Excellent Dairy with Slate Shelves, white Tiled Walls and Tiled floor.

Kitchen, 17-ft. by 15-ft. with 7-ft. 6-in. Close Range, two Ovens and Hot Plate and Linen-airing Cupboard at side.

Back Kitchen – a 6-ft. 6-in. Hot Plate with Oven and Boiler and large Coal Hole.

IN THE BASEMENT

Fine Cellarage with Gas laid on, extending the whole length of Hotel, comprising Wine and Spirit Cellar, enclosed Inner Wine Cellar. Beer Cellar, enclosed Mineral Water Cellar, etc.

IN THE YARD, under the Assembly Room is

A Wine Store 24-ft. 6-in. by 17-ft.

A Large Room now used as a Store 46-ft. by 18-ft.

ON THE FIRST FLOOR

The Private Wing, with separate Staircase and Staircase from Offices, comprising

Billiard Room 25-ft. 6-in. by 17-ft. with movable boarded partition, dividing it into two Rooms,

Sitting Room 18-ft. 9-in. by 13-ft 3-in.

Good Store Cupboard

On the Staircase leading to this Wing are folding doors communicating with Room No. 7, by which the Ballroom can by reached, without descending to the Ground-floor.

IN THE MAIN BUILDING is

A Handsome and Lofty Ballroom, measuring 53-ft. 6-in. by 23-ft. 6-in., used also as a Cyclists' Tea and Reception Room, with Two Fireplaces and excellent Slow Combustion Stoves, the Ceiling is arched being 15-ft. 3-in. high in the centre. Beside the approach through the Main Corridor, there is a separate Stairway from Yard, affording an entrance without going through the Hotel.

Room No.	1	Bedroom	14-ft. 0-in. by 12-ft. 3-in.
"	2	"	10-ft. 9-in. by 10-ft. 7-in.
"	3	"	14-ft. 4-in. by 10-ft. 8-in.
		adjoining and communicating with	
"	4	A fine Sitting Room	26-ft. 9-in. by 15-ft. 10-in.
Room No.	5	Sitting Room	15-ft. 6-in. by 11-ft. 9-in.
"	6	Bedroom	19-ft. 6-in. by 15-ft. 6-in.
"	7	Small Bedroom or Dressing Room	12-ft. 0-in. by 10-ft. 6-in.
		communicating by folding doors with Billiard Room Wing.	
"	8	Bedroom	12-ft. 6-in. by 11-ft. 0-in.
		A suite of Four Rooms, viz:–	
"	9	Bedroom	15-ft. 10-in. by 11-ft. 0-in.
"	10	"	11-ft. 0-in. by 11-ft. 0-in.
"	11	"	11-ft. 0-in. by 11-ft. 0-in.
"	12	Dressing Room communicating with either Rooms 9 or 11	

Water is laid on just outside this Wing in the Passage, where there is also a useful Store Cupboard.

ON THE SECOND FLOOR

Are eight Servants' Bedrooms, one being approached by a separate Staircase.

THE UPPER YARD

is approached by a Covered Archway from the Main Street, and is surrounded by the following Buildings

Harness Room, Enclosed Double Coachhouse with two pairs folding Doors.

A 6-stall Stable.

A Range of Four Loose Boxes

Ostler's Room

A 6-stall Stable with Hay Bin

IN THE LOWER YARD

Open-front Coach House, 25-ft. by 12-ft.

Bottle Shed and Wood Shed

A 4-stall Stable with Meal Room adjoining and Pigstye.

A Carriage House with folding Doors and an open lean-to Van House

An open-front Carriage House 30-ft. by 20-ft.

An Enclosed Carriage House, 32-ft. by 20-ft., with double folding doors and Pigeon House over

A 4-Stall Stable with Fodder Store or Pony Stall at end.

Adjoining is

A Small Enclosed Farm Yard
in which Water is laid on, surrounded by the following Buildings:–

A Loose Box and two Buildings used as Cow Stalls, a Building with 5 Stalls, 2 Loose Boxes, a Covered Shed and small Hay Stall at end, which with a little alteration would make very convenient accommodation for Polo Ponies, for which there is a great demand in the Village.

There is a

Large Garden.
Well Stocked with Fruit Trees
Having a
Heated Cucumber House 27-ft. 6-in. by 8-ft. 6-in.,
and a Span-Roof Greenhouse 20-ft. by 13-ft.

'The Swan' Tap

Is situated on the upper side of the Yard Entrance to the Hotel and contains the following accommodation:-

Public Bar 15-ft. 6-in. by 11-ft. 3-in.
Parlour and Bagatelle Room with Serving Hatch from Bar 23-ft. by 11-ft. 6-in.
Tap Room 11-ft. 6-in. by 9-ft. 6-in.
Store Room at rear of Bar.
Side Entrance from Swan Brewery Yard.
Parlour. Kitchen with Sink, and Water laid on.
Wood Shed, W.C., and small Paved Yard at side.
Two Bedrooms on First Floor
A large and capital Beer Cellar with Entrance from the Yard.

The whole property has the commanding Frontage of 117-ft. 6-in. on the Main Street, in the very Centre of the Town, where all the Approach Roads meet.

The Furniture, Fixtures, Trade Fixtures and Utensils, Stock, Horses, Carriages, Harness etc. etc. are to be taken and paid for by the purchaser at a valuation to be made by two valuers or their umpire in the usual way, in addition to the purchase-money, in accordance with an Inventory to be produced at the time of Sale.

The Hotel is supplied with Water for all internal purposes by an old arrangement with the Swan Brewery from the deep well on the Brewery Premises, on the payment by the occupier of this property of 1s. per 1,000 gallons for pumping. The Stabling and other Outbuildings have the use of all the Waste Water from the above Brewery free of charge.

Owners of the Swan

Owners from 1637 until possession by the Moore family in 1858

1637   Owned by Thomas Goodman, husband of Olive.
Tenant Miss Brown, and later Nicholas Brown.
Swan Inn passed to Mary, their daughter, on her marriage to John Barfoote.

1681   The Will of Mary Barfoote gave all her lands to her grandson, John Barfoote.

1693   Edward Toy

1713   Edward Toy

1726   Edward Toy bought the freehold. Tenant was John Toy, his son.

1784   Tenant Mrs. Ives.

23.6.1784   Ann Toy, widow of John, and Richard Toy, only child of Ann and John, sold to Edward Rowley of Parish of St. Mary, Lambeth.

1789   Mary, wife of Edward Rowley, died.

1791   Edward Rowley died.

22.11.1794   Their Daughter, Anne Jane Rowley, married Thomas Ede of Dorking; they had three children –

(1) James Charles Rowley Ede, baptised at St. Mary, Lambeth on 22.9.1799 and by 1831 was married to Hester.

(2) Ann Harriet, who married William Baiment, was born on 27.11.1795.

(3) Thomas Ede, buried 11.10.1806 aged 7 months.

1791   On death of Edward Rowley, Ann Harriet Baiment, née Ede, and James Charles Rowley Ede, brother and sister, inherited the Swan in equal shares. Tenant was George Scroggs.

1820   Ann Jane Ede, née Rowley, was buried at Islington, Middlesex, aged 48.

1820   James Rowley Ede of Lombard St. London, and Ann Harriet Ede of Lambeth, then spinster, let the premises for 21 years to George Scroggs of Southwark whose sub-tenant was John Jones.

1824   Ann Harriet Ede and William Baiment had four children.
   (1) William Edward Baiment of 1 Garden Cottages, Picton St., Camberwell, a baker.
   (2) James Baiment of Leigh Farm, a labourer.
   (3) George Heseltine Baiment, a labourer.
   (4) Ann Harriet Baiment of 77 Fleet St., London, spinster.

1838   James Charles Rowley Ede, and his wife Hester, sold their share in the Swan to Edward Collins, brewer of Richmond, and John Downs of Richmond.

1849   George Scroggs who had a further lease, surrendered it to the four children of Ann Harriet Baiment née Ede and William Baiment.

1850   William Edward Baiment and James Baiment, the two eldest children of Ann Harriet Baiment, sold their quarter share in the Swan to William Moore.

1852   Ann Harriet Baiment sold her one eighth share to William Moore.

1856   George Heseltine Baiment sold his one eighth share to William Moore.

1858   The Executors of Edward Collins and John Downs sold their half share to William Moore.

Further owners of the Swan were:–

1898   George Brown
1908   Henry Flower
1909   J. Lack
1911   William Charles Ginder
1915   Arthur George Davey
1919   Mrs. Mary Jane Davey
1926–29 Edwin H. Gilbert
1934   George Laceby

The Swan Brewery

The Brewery dated from 1859 when it was founded by William Moore who owned the Swan Hotel. From 1871–1874 it was under the control of his wife Emily, and in 1875 was transferred to George Moore & Co., George being their son. The new Steam Brewery was built in 1874 – the smell of the brewing by now filling the air in the centre of Leatherhead. The new building was on land adjoining the hotel and was opened in 1875. The builder was a local man, Mr. Felix Walker. The building was described then as Italian style, of red brick and concrete, with blue and white moulded brick enrichments. The cellar walls, arches, walls and floor of the tun room were of concrete and the lime used for this and throughout the building was patent selenitic, all being considerably cheaper than brickwork. The chimney was of red, white and blue brick with encaustic tile bands.

The frontage to the High Street was about 60 feet and the premises to the rear formed a regular quadrangle of about 250 feet in depth. The Brewery was constructed on the tower principle. On the ground floor of the tower were the engine-room and mill-room, the second floor was used as a malt store and the third floor was a mash room containing a twelve-quarter mesh tun, malt hopper and three tanks for hot and cold water with an aggregate capacity of four thousand gallons. The tun room adjoined the tower block and was used for racking the beer and also contained the yeast wagons which caught the yeast from the fermenting vessels placed in the room above, called the fermenting room. There were eventually eight fermenting vessels. From here led off the stillion room used for storing beers in larger casks as they were racked – storage was for some five hundred barrels which were let down to the cellar by lift. The cellars were extensive, both under the tower, extending to an area under the Swan Yard, and under the Swan stables. A private road led to stabling with a loft over and more cellars underneath. This roadway was later partly covered.

Panoramic drawing of the Swan Brewery which was incorporated in a large advertisement, c.1903–1921. The houses in the Fairfield can be seen in the distance

41

The Swan Brewery staff, 1920

To ensure that the water used was absolutely pure, the supply came from an artesian tube bore, sunk to a depth of 200 feet into the chalk, with a steel tube in its entire length checked periodically by chemical and bacteriological tests.

In mid-December 1903 there was very heavy rainfall which percolated into the underground storage reservoir and a check then certified that the water was 'suitable for the production of high class ales'.

For cooling purposes there was a shallow well from which four thousand gallons of water per hour was lifted by a Worthington pump into a large tank – this could be used immediately in any outbreak of fire.

By 1904 the popularity of the beer was such that new machinery was being fitted. Pale ales were the chief products, but stout and porter were also brewed, though not extensively. The best available malt and hops were used – only English and mostly from Kent and Worcester.

The area covered by the distribution from the Brewery was about 12 miles – Redhill, Reigate, Ockley, Dorking, Gomshall and Shere, Guildford, Cobham, Hersham, Thames Ditton, Epsom, Ewell, Sutton and Chessington. The Brewery had houses at

The Brewery offices

Hersham, Sutton, Epsom, Ewell, Dorking and Tadworth as well as owning in Leatherhead the 'Plough', the 'Running Horse', the 'Swan Hotel' and the 'Jug House' in Church Street.

The Brewery had, from 1876, been under the control of W.B. Heaver, managing partner of George Moore & Co., who was also a local resident and was instrumental in making the Swan Brewery Co. such a successful business.

On his retirement the business passed by sale to a private syndicate of local gentlemen and was under their General Manager, J.W. James, another local man who had worked under Mr. Heaver.

Four other breweries in the neighbourhood were taken over – two of these, Dagnalls of Epsom and Lucocks of Dorking, during the management of George Moore, and a further two, Boxalls of Dorking and Sayers of Ashtead, after J.W. James took over the management.

The White Horse Brewery at Epsom, run by Charles Dagnall, was acquired in 1885, as a going concern. The Rock Brewery, Dorking, owned by the Lucock family, was acquired by William Moore in 1890, and retained by the Moore family as personal estate, and was only conveyed to the Swan Brewery Co. Ltd. in 1903 on a 31 year lease.

Boxall & Sons' Sun Brewery, Dorking was acquired in 1907, including 8 public houses when W.T. Boxall, its owner, took a seat on the board of directors.

Sayers' Ashtead Brewery and its four public houses were leased to the Swan Brewery Co. Ltd. in 1913 who immediately closed down the brewing operations at Ashtead. Their public houses were supplied from Leatherhead, and a mineral water factory was established on the site.

By the beginning of the 20th century the Brewery was the leading commercial industry of the town, having a high reputation for its products, and providing much local employment and prosperity. About twenty five were employed including clerks, draymen, cellarmen and bottlers, the wages bill coming to approximately £2,000 p.a., nearly all spent in Leatherhead. It was estimated that about 150 men, women and children were dependent on the Brewery for their daily bread. Extra men were taken on to keep the premises clean and the Brewery Company was quoted as saying that, 'property had its duties as well as rights, and a great deal of money was being spent on all their properties throughout their district so that the tenants may have every convenience and accommodation for themselves as well as for their customers'.

The Leatherhead Urban District Council had taken part of the ground and first floors of the new Brewery offices and further rooms were let off to various professional men including also the Surveyors Department of the Council.

Even as late as post Second World War there were still barrel rests in an upstairs room and a beam and pulley at the back of the building.

In 1893 a new brick church was built by the Methodists in Church Road and their original iron chapel continued in use as a schoolroom. In 1904 it was sold to the Brewery for £27.10.0d. and was erected behind their premises

A terra-cotta slab from the Brewery building

From 1903–1921 the Brewery was known as the Swan Brewery Co. Ltd. In September 1903 the Brewery was offered for sale with 21 public houses, but did not find a buyer and was withdrawn at £64,500. However, in the October of the same year it was sold by private treaty to J.W.James, who had been the manager, for a sum close to £64,500. On the 1st of that month the Brewery was registered as the Swan Brewery Leatherhead Company Ltd. with a capital of £50,000 in £100 shares to 'acquire and carry on the Swan Brewery and Hotel with 19 public houses and to continue the business still carried on by George Moore & Co. as brewers, maltsters and wine and spirits merchants'. The directors were F. Hue Williams of the London Stock Exchange, Chairman, H. Moore and J.W. James. The qualification was £1,000.

Just before the start of the First World War a boy from Bookham named Turville Kille, started work at the Brewery, soon after he left school. He worked a twelve hour day, starting at six in the morning, earning just one pound a week.

The Swan from the hotel porch, now in the garden of Leatherhead Museum

In a book telling of his life and times he describes his time working there.

'Behind the brewery was a boiler that supplied the steam for blowing the whistle which told the workers when it was time to start or finish work. It was blown four times a day and it could be heard in Bookham when the wind was blowing in the right direction.

I had the job of removing the empties from the crates which contained four quart bottles or two dozen pint bottles. Sometimes, when I turned the crates upside down, money would fall out. When this happened I'd put my foot on it, then look around, and if the coast was clear, I'd pick it up and put it in my pocket. You were supposed to share any money that was found. I also had to remove the screw stoppers from the bottles and sniff them to see if they'd been used for paraffin, in which case they would be put aside for special treatment.

Next to the boiler house was a galvanised tank into which hot water was pumped from the boiler. The bottles would be immersed in the water and removed by hand and then pushed onto rotating brushes over the tank.

Once the insides had been cleaned, the bottles would go into a rinsing tank, then be removed and placed upside down in the crates to dry.

Wearing thick black aprons we'd sit side by side when, using a bottle-filling machine, we filled the bottles from the barrels which rested on a platform above us. Once the stoppers had been put in and the Swan Brewery's labels stuck on, the bottles went into the crates, which would be stacked in different places till they were ready to be delivered to the Swan Brewery pubs. Sometimes, when the foreman wasn't around, the men would come down to where we were doing the bottling and help themselves to a bottle. I had to load the crates onto the dray and help the drayman deliver them to the pubs in the district. The beer in the barrels was brewed by specially trained men'.

Turville left the Brewery in 1914 at the age of 16.

The entire business was acquired by Mellersh & Neale on 2nd November 1921 and closed at the end of that year. The whole site was redeveloped in 1936 when the Swan Hotel was demolished. Some of the cellars had been filled in by the Council in 1932, though some remained to be used as air-raid shelters during the war. The deserted yard was used as a playground by local boys, one of whom remembers the barrels and staves left there, and one deep remaining hole. A farm gate was still at the back end of the yard leading to the public path.

The Brewery office building remained as Barclays Bank and later a betting office with the rest of the building still being used as offices until the redevelopment of the Swan Centre in the 1970's. Two of the terracotta panels with flower designs have been incorporated into the wall of No. 31 High Street.